NEW AND CURIOUS SCHOOL
OF THEATRICAL DANCING

NEW AND CURIOUS
SCHOOL of THEATRICAL
DANCING

By
GREGORIO LAMBRANZI

With all the Original Plates
By JOHANN GEORG PUSCHNER

Translated from the German
By DERRA DE MORODA

Edited with a Preface
By CYRIL W. BEAUMONT

One of a series of republications by
Dance Horizons, Incorporated
1801 East 26th Street, Brooklyn, New York 11229

*The typography used is that arranged by Cyril W. Beaumont for the first
English edition, edited and published by him in London, in 1928, for
The Imperial Society of Teachers of Dancing.*

PREFACE

THIS book which, to the best of my knowledge, is now reprinted for the first time, is one of the rarest works on dancing. It was issued in two parts, both published at Nuremberg in 1716, by Johann Jacob Wolrab.

Part I. contains a decorative title-page, which forms the frontispiece to the present volume, five pages of text and fifty plates, engraved throughout. The text consists of the author's foreword in German and Italian, a brief description of the work in the same languages, and an Italian version of the directions engraved on each plate.

Part II., which is excessively rare, contains a decorative title-page and fifty-one plates, engraved throughout. There is no text save that engraved on the plates. In the present reprint the plates have been slightly reduced, those in the original edition measuring 8.6 by 6.3 inches.

I have been unable to glean any information regarding the author, Gregorio Lambranzi, beyond what he tells us himself ; namely, that he was a Venetian *maître de ballet*. Obviously he lived during the end of the seventeenth and beginning of the eighteenth centuries, and it is clear from this work that he must have been gifted with a lively imagination and considerable creative ability, and risen to eminence in his profession.

There is a similar dearth of particulars regarding the career of Johann Georg Puschner, the artist who drew and engraved these plates. All the artistic biographies speak with a like brevity and state simply that he was born probably at Nuremberg, where he flourished from 1670 to 1720.

I cannot convey the excitement that possessed me when I discovered, some years ago, a copy of this work in the British Museum catalogued under early music. Nor can I express the delight and quickening anticipation with which I turned over the plates. Even now I have only to look through the book to imagine myself seated in some eighteenth century theatre, watching these lively dancers glide and step, jump and stamp, twirl and bounce before my eyes. Is there any other book in the world which contains such marvellous character dances ?

The author's plan is quite unusual. Instead of making use of the Feuillet system of stenochoregraphy, or some analogous method, by which to record his dances, he gives the theme and air for each, suggestions for steps, and, by means of an engraving, conveys the style-atmosphere and setting of the dance, and the costume to be worn.

From such indications the professional reader is expected to be able to arrange a dance. True, this presupposes a certain power of invention and an instinct for style ; but the plan of giving a rough outline and leaving the dancer to fill in the details, is worthy of emulation. It permits the composer to interpret the theme in his own manner and create a living thing. This is far preferable to the laborious deciphering of signs which, however well they may preserve the skeleton, cannot endow it with life.

What a different state of affairs obtains in Lambranzi's method! The artist, with the author to serve him as model, has really succeeded in conveying not only the manner in which the dancer stood, but the way in which he moved. The head, face, arms, body and legs—all are expressive to a degree ; and every pose is distinguished by a nice feeling for line. Mark, too, how the style of dance changes with the subject. Each has a distinct and definite character of its own. Everything Lambranzi saw seems to have been a source of inspiration to him, and it is certain that the dances given represent only a tithe of all those he devised. I feel that his career might be summed up in a paraphase of Cæsar's *Veni, Vidi, Vici* : I came, I saw, I composed a dance.

The themes are full of ingenuity and variety. There are suggestions which range from light comedy to a full-flavoured buffoonery that is obviously inspired by the recollection of scenes from the *Commedia dell' Arte*. Many of the traditional Masks themselves appear : Harlequin, Scaramouch, Purricinella, Pantalone, Scapino, Fenocchio, Mezzetino, the Bolognese Doctor and Narcisino. All these are strongly marked types with special characteristics of their own, which at once prompt the style-atmosphere of the dance.

To make this point clear, consider a modern Mask, such as Charlie Chaplin, created by Mr. Charles Chaplin. This great actor has a number of characteristic movements and poses which, through the popularity of the films in which he appears, are familiar to everyone. Any person possessed of a knowledge of dancing could interpret a simple theme in the manner of Charlie Chaplin because he or she would have a definite idea as to how that actor would walk, or run, or act under various conditions. Thus it would only be necessary to arrange a series of steps and actions to express the given theme, and then to revise them in terms of Charlie Chaplin. These dances depend on the application of the same principle.

Doubtless many readers will be well acquainted with the characteristics of the Masks mentioned. For those who are not, it may be helpful briefly to define their origin and qualities. The Masks, or fixed characters, were derived from all the provinces of Italy. The four chief and oldest Masks were Arlecchino (Harlequin), Brighella, Pantalone and Il Dottore

(The Doctor). The first two were natives of Bergamo, the third came from Venice, and the last from Bologna.

The best portrait of Harlequin in the eighteenth century is that painted by Marmontel, who says of him :

" His character presents a mixture of ignorance, *naiveté*, stupidity and grace. He is like a mere sketch of a man, a great child visited by flashes of reason and intelligence, in all of whose capers and awkwardnesses there is something sharp and interesting. The model Harlequin is all suppleness and agility, with the grace of a young cat, yet equipped with a superficial coarseness that renders his performances more amusing ; the part is that of a lackey, patient, faithful, credulous, gluttonous, always in love, always in difficulties on his master's account or his own, afflicting himself and consoling himself again with the readiness of a child, one whose sorrows are as amusing as his joys. Such a part demands a great deal of naturalness and of wit, and a great deal of physical grace and suppleness."

Brighella is a sly rogue, a dangerous rascal with an ingratiating manner. The forerunner of the confidence trickster, he has no scruples as to the use of perjury or theft. Lively and insolent with women, a boaster with old men and weaklings, he is the first to take flight when difficulty arises or danger threatens. But this will not prevent his dealing a stab in the back if opportunity permits and necessity requires it. Skilled in flattery, able to sing, play and dance, he is unmatched at making himself a welcome, if uninvited guest. In short, he is a prince of wheedlers.

Scapino, Fenocchio, Mezzetino and Narcisino are all variants of Brighella. Fenocchio made his appearance on the Italian stage as early as 1560. He is usually employed in amorous intrigue. Scapino, as his name which is derived from *scappare*, to escape, suggests, is more cowardly than Brighella. He shudders at the very thought of using violence. Mezzetino is the same kind of shrewd lackey, working for himself or acting as servant to gay philanderers such as Ottavio and Cinthio, or playing the deceived or deceiving husband. Narcisino is a native of Malalbergo, a town between Bologna and Ferrara. He generally takes the part of a stupid servant, or that of a foolish and self-willed father or guardian.

Pantalone is a father, husband, widower or old bachelor. He can be either rich or poor, but is invariably avaricious and mistrustful, and often ridiculous.

The Doctor is the learned man caricatured. He can talk on any subject and at such length that his audience either falls asleep or departs long before the oration has ended. He cannot discuss the simplest matter without the introduction of Latin tags.

Purricinella is the Bolognese variant of Pulcinella. He is coarse and stupid as opposed to the wit and astuteness of the latter.

Scaramouch is derived from the Italian *scaramuzzia*, meaning a little fighter or skirmisher, and this Mask is a descendant of the ancient figure of Comedy known as the Captain, who is a braggart, a boaster and a liar. He breathes hell-fire and slaughter. But if his victim's eyebrow but frowns or his hand strays to his sword-hilt, then the Captain's courage evaporates like the gas from a pricked toy balloon. He concocts so many legends of his prowess that by sheer force of repetition he ends by believing them himself. In war he outrivals the exploits of Bayard ; in love, his amorous propensities would put to shame those of Casanova.

Then there are dances suggested by various professions and trades ; a pikeman going through his postures, a platoon of grenadiers at drill, a cobbler waxing his thread, coopers driving hoops on a barrel, blacksmiths forging a nail, a tailor measuring a customer for a dress. Sports and pastimes are likewise the themes of dances. And lastly there is a long dance where the movements are frankly acrobatic, they smack of the tumbler rather than the dancer.

It is safe to assume that the majority of dance teachers and dancers who will compose these dances will adapt *pas* with which they are familiar to the exigencies of the theme, the known or imagined qualities of the character, and the general style-atmosphere gleaned from an examination of the plate or plates. Those, however, who seek a knowledge of the manner in which the basic *pas* were executed in the early eighteenth century will find all their questions answered in these three books : Feuillet (R. A.), *Choregraphie* (1701) ; Rameau (P.), *Le Maître à danser* (1725), and *Abbregé de la nouvelle methode* (1725).

One movement, however, does present a little difficulty ; that is the term *pirole*. This word occurs eight times throughout the plates as follows : Part I. *Pirole* (1), *Piroleten* (19, 24, 25) ; Part II. *Piroles* (2), *Birollets* (25), *Pirole* (37), and *Birolle* (39). In general this word seems to mean *pirouette*, and I think is rightly so translated. I cannot trace the word *pirole* in any French, German, Italian or Spanish dictionary. This turning movement is *pirouette* in French and German, *piroetta* in Italian, and *pirueta* in Spanish. The nearest approach to *pirole* that I have been able to find is the Italian *pirolo*, meaning a peg or pin ; and it may be that *pirole* is derived from it, unless it is a dialect word, or simply a case of misspelling.

That this last conjecture is within the bounds of possibility is clearly proved by the author's use of the term *Stehpas*, in the German preface, which obviously means *jeté pas*. This is a mistake that has persisted for years, due to some pupils having never been taught the meaning and correct spelling of terms in daily use. In comparatively recent publications I have seen the word *jeté* written as " stay." There is one instance, plate 37 of Part II., where *pirouette* does not seem to be the equivalent of *pirole*, for the *pas* represented suggests the Russian *prisiadka* step, better known as the " cobbler " step.

The settings for the dances are very interesting. In general they consist of three or four pairs of " wings " and a backcloth. They are comparatively simple, far removed from the elaborate architectural conceptions, with their rich baroque ornaments, of such masters as the Bibienas, Juvarra and Piranesi. Nearly all are designed on vertical lines, possibly to enhance the curved lines presented by the movements of the dancers.

These scenes have one great merit in that they leave the stage free for the dancers. Representational scenery is generally distasteful in colour, but it might be an interesting experiment to set dancers in coloured costumes, not too high in key, against such style of scenery as in these plates, but painted in monotone, to suggest an etching or engraving.

As the reader turns over the enchanted pages of this book he will be impressed by two things. First, the ingenuity, resource and originality possessed by the author. Second, the extreme difficulty of accomplishing anything really new. When Nijinsky produced *Jeux* in 1913, the idea of using a branch of sport as a theme for ballet was acclaimed as a stroke of genius. Yet here is a dance of tennis-players produced almost two hundred years ago ! In the acrobatic dance which is given towards the end of Part II., look at No. 47. Does this not suggest the work of Massine in his latest ballet *Ode ?* Consider No. 48; does this not recall his *Pulcinella ?*

I have dwelt somewhat on this point, because I regard the study of dance literature as an important part of the dancer's education, and one far too often neglected. So many dancers, alas, believe the physical training to be the *alpha* and *omega* of their art. And what after all is the purpose of this training ? First and foremost to make the body malleable, to make it plastic, so that when the mind commands the limbs to perform a certain movement, they are fitted with the requisite strength and balance to obey on the instant.

In the hands of a good teacher, any person, of suitable age

and endowed with the right kind of body, can acquire the graces and physical abilities which mark the well-trained dancer. A certain amount of personality, if inherent, may be developed. A certain professional ease of manner may be gained from appearing before the public. But, from the purely dancing standpoint, there is little difference between such a dancer and a hundred others who have been similarly trained. They might all have been stamped from the same die. And, as a general rule, the young woman who on the completion of her physical training is honestly convinced that she is a finished dancer, more—an artist, is nothing but a beautiful machine, a robot.

The truth is that while the dancer's body has been educated, often to excess, her mind has been left to vegetate. What does she know of the history of dancing, of the great dancers of the past, of style-atmosphere, of costume ? A few dates, a few names, and that is all. It is a common failing with dancers to regard books as dull, useless things which harbour dust and take up room ; prints and engravings are treated with a little courtesy simply because they may serve to decorate the walls of the studio.

This attitude of indifference must be changed. Not only must books be read and their message be assimilated, and prints and engravings be studied, but this knowledge must be distilled, and re-distilled, and preserved with care. Faust bartered his soul for a brief renewal of his youth. Here is a better bargain. The power to become an artist in exchange for a short period of daily study. Look at the visions imprisoned in this casket. Who so cold but cannot thrill at the sight of them ? Study them and they will be bound to your will. And as you continue your studies, you will command more and more visions. To you they will yield up their secrets, that rare knowledge which goes so far towards transforming the dancer into the artist.

CYRIL W. BEAUMONT

The Author's Foreword

A S these illustrations of my theatrical dances, for which I myself served as the model, have succeeded better than I had anticipated, I feel it my duty to publish them as so many persons have requested ; for these and similar dances greatly stimulate and delight the lover of dancing. Hence such dances are generally styled *Delicium Populi*, or the People's Delight.

My aim is not to describe in detail the choregraphy of these dances or any particular *pas*, still less to depict all their possible variations ; this would be too ambitious a work and, moreover, would necessitate a large volume. But, by means of the illustration and its accompanying air, the majority of which are my own compositions, I shall portray a principal character in appropriate costume, the style of his dance and the manner of its execution. I shall also explain the essential matters in such illustrations and indicate what *pas* should be employed.

However, it is not my intention to restrict anyone to my method but to leave each dancer free to adapt it as he pleases. For those requiring information I shall state that Spanish *pas* are used for Nos. 1 to 3, Roman *pas* for Nos. 21 and 22, and all kinds of *cabrioles* such as those from one side to the other, forwards and backwards, *coupés, jetés, chassés, pas graves, contretemps, pas de chaconne, pas de courante* and other similar *pas* according to the directions given below each illustration. For the peasant dances in Nos. 4 to 12, all *pas de gavotte* and *chassés* are required, besides the French *pas de menuet ;* also *pas de bourrée* and certain peasant *contretemps, gosi* [?] on either foot, *pas de glospied*[1] [?], *pas de rigaudon* and *balancés*.

The lively and burlesque types represented in Nos. 23 to 49, such as Scaramouch, Harlequin and the like, must be expressed in the eccentric style of dancing ; and with, of course, ridiculous and comic positions suited to the peculiar characteristics of each. Hence it would be quite out of place for a Scaramouch, Harlequin or Purricinella to dance a *Menuet*, *Courante*, *Sarabande* or *Entrée*, since each has his own droll and quaint *pas*. Thus Scaramouch dances his long, unformed and heavy imitations such as the *pas de scaramouche ;* the same applies to Harlequin, Mezzetino, Scapino, Matto, the Bolognese Doctor, Narcisino, Fenocchio, Orbo, Zotto, Strupiato, Pantalone and so on. For these, no *pas*, figure or costume can be used other than that usually employed on the Italian stage ; nevertheless each dancer should be allowed full play to his powers of invention.

In conclusion, I can assure the reader that I have myself performed these dances in the most distinguished theatres of Germany, Italy and France, and that nearly all are my own compositions. If this work is received with favour, I shall give to the world further new and extraordinary creations to prove the extent of the knowledge I have acquired, and of which there is an abundance to impart to others.

FAREWELL

---

[1] Perhaps this is a misspelling of *clos-pied*, and is a jump with the feet held together.

PART ONE

Part One

A Description of the Plates

1. This is the first position or preparation for a *cabriole* to the left. It is followed by one to the right. The other *pas*, such as the *pirole* [*pirouette* ?], *pas de rigaudon* and *coupé*, can be found in the Foreword, so that it should be quite easy for anyone to compose the whole dance.

2. This dance begins with a *coupé* which is followed by *pas tombés*, *pas de sissonne* and *pas de bourrée*. The rest of this *Sarabande* can be arranged at pleasure.

3. In this dance *pas de courante*, *pas graves*, *ballonnés*, *pas de sissonne* and *pas de chaconne* must be employed, together with such other *pas* as the dancer may select.

4. This plate represents the first peasant step. It is then done the opposite way with the other foot, and succeeded by *contretemps* and *pas de rigaudon*, with a drawing to and fro of the arms, knees and legs, but in divers manners in peasant style.

5. After the couple shown have performed half the dance, the woman steals away ; and since the man no longer sees her, he begins to cry. But, unperceived, she returns and, going behind him, takes hold of his shoulders and turns him round several times. And because she sees him crying they begin to dance again.

6. This peasant dance is begun by the man alone. At the end of the air the woman enters with a broom, with which she belabours the man and drives him away. Now he comes back

and attacks her in turn, but as she vigorously repulses him they achieve a ridiculous dance with these alternate blows and then both run off.

7. Enter a man and woman who threaten each other with wooden platters, which they clash together in time with the music, always turning themselves round. At last they embrace and throw away the platters, when the dance comes to an end.

8. This dance represents two peasants in love. At the beginning they push each other with their elbows and heels. then continue the dance with various other actions to the end of the air, which can be repeated twice or three times at pleasure.

9. Here we see two persons performing a dance of friendship. When they have fanned themselves with their hats and scratched their heads, while alternately drawing back their shoulders and legs, they perform all manner of droll antics in time with the music, and the dance comes to an end.

10. When the curtain is raised this drunken peasant is seen. As the air begins he tries to get up, but falls down several times. At last he staggers to his feet and waves his hand to the tankard of beer, which does not want to come to him. Reeling, he snatches it up, drinks from it thrice, puts it on the ground again and finishes the strain by staggering backwards and forwards, walking and jumping. At the end he claps on his hat, picks up the tankard and exits tottering from side to side.

11. A drunken peasant staggers in with a tankard. When the air has been played once, his wife enters and seeing him so drunk, slaps her knee with astonishment. But the man gives her the tankard to drink from and, when she has done so, they dance about in a drunken manner. But the woman pretends that she can still dance and so they continue until they lose sight of each other.

12. Two peasant boys begin to dance. When the air has been played once, two peasant men enter and laugh at them and blow through their noses at the same time. Since the

boys do likewise the men jog them with their knees and elbows. The boys retaliate in the same manner, and so the men try to prevent their dancing. At last they become reconciled, all dance together and at the end run off with merry gestures.

13. A Roman sailor does certain *ballonnés* backwards and some *pas de bourrée* forwards. Then he performs *pas de rigaudon* and *chassés* with various contortions and swings of the arms. He exits when the air has been played once.

14. The same sailor dances in from the " wings " with his wife, and when he has let her pass several times under his arm, as if catching her, as shown in the plate, they dance towards each other, using the air marked No. 13. At the end they embrace and exit dancing.

15. Here two old women enter and dance, half-walking, half-shaking, as far as possible to the extreme front of the stage. Then they scratch themselves before and behind, spin round and go back to whence they began, with their backs to the audience, where they perform the same gestures. These goings backwards and forwards continue until the end of the first air. Meanwhile a youth enters who, on seeing the old women, laughs at them. And when their air has ended, he takes each in turn by the hand and drags them by the arm, until his air has been danced twice or three times.

It is to be observed that the dance consists of two airs, the first of which is slow, while the other is merry and quick.

16. These two Masks, who represent four persons, dance gravely and almost with difficulty ; now from one side to the other, now forwards, now backwards, now in a circle ; in such a manner that each appears to carry another person on his back. And this continues for so long as the dancers please.

17. A satyr performs *ballonnés* until the violin comes to the sign △ in the air. Then the satyr blows his pipes and the woman plays her tambourine in accompaniment. When the sign has been passed he again dances until the sign □ is

reached, when they again use the pipes and tambourine ; he to blow and she to play in harmony with the bowing of the violin, and this is done whenever they come to the signs. The air can be repeated as often as desired.

18. This masked peasant stands inside a basket without a bottom[1] and performs the *pas de rigaudon*, with strong stamps of the foot on the ground. Then he takes the position shown above and performs *ballonnés* and *contretemps* in a peasant, though technically correct, manner. Meanwhile the air is played four times.

19. When the curtain rises we see a man with two faces. First, always looking upwards, he dances forwards with *cabrioles*, *pirouettes*[2] and other Spanish *pas*. Then he stands with his back to the audience and displays his other face, with the back of his costume fashioned like the front. In the same manner he does various other *cabrioles*, and exits when the air has been played three times.

20. Enter the same dancer with a woman,[3] one from one side and one from the other. Soon they dance together with joined hands and continually turn their heads to and fro. Then they quickly run apart. This is done alternately so that sometimes they dance together and sometimes apart. The air is played three times.

21. A Roman performs a *cabriole* forwards quickly followed by another backwards, and then one to the side. As for the rest of the dance everyone will compose for themselves a few beautiful *enchaînements* of French *pas*. The air is played three times.

22. Here the *pas de courante*, *pas de bourrée* and *pas de*

---

[1] The man is wearing a woman's skirt. The woman's head and shoulders is a dummy figure attached to the basket.

[2] The German gives *piroleten*.

[3] Note that the woman also wears a mask on the back of her head to suggest she has two faces.

chaconne are danced in Roman costume, with pretty movements of the arms, head and body. The air is played twice.

23. When the curtain rises this ridiculous person is seen at the back of the stage. Gradually coming to the front he regains his true height. Then he throws the cloak behind him, jumps upwards, keeping his knees straight and stretching his legs as far apart as possible, and comes to the ground with his knees straight. After this he performs quite easily the long *pas de scaramouche*[1] with *cabrioles* in a different manner until the air ends.

24. When the curtain rises there is revealed this lovely figure which remains like a statue until the first part of the air has been played. When this is repeated Scaramouch jumps off his pedestal and performs his beautiful *pas de scaramouche*, with *cabrioles* and *pirouettes*.[2] The dance ends when the air has been played three times.

25. This plate shows how Scaramouch enters and performs long steps combined with *cabrioles* and *pirouettes*,[2] and dances likewise according to the instructions so often given.

26. Scaramouch enters with two baskets, each containing a smaller Scaramouch, which he sets down. When he has danced the whole of the air once, the small Scaramouches open the baskets, which greatly surprises him. They jump out, kick him from behind and push him to the ground. Then they dance the whole of the air themselves. Afterwards Scaramouch, having got up, catches first one then the other, and forces them back into their baskets. This ends the first half of the air. During the second half he takes up the baskets and exits with long strides.

27. These two persons jump from the " wings " and take up the position shown above at the end of the first part of the

---

[1] The *pas de scaramouche* appears to be a long stride, so exaggerated that the body is almost touching the ground.

[2] The German is *piroleten*.

air. At the beginning of the second part they jump back into the " wings."

28. Of these persons nothing can be seen but the hat and foot. When the air has been played three or four times, they alter their positions and resume the first with different *cabrioles.* Then they exit.

29. Harlequin enters as shown and begins to dance step by step in his own manner. Then Scaramouch approaches him with a lantern, dances and mimics him, but finally resolves to go away.

30. Scaramouch enters muffled up in a cloak and bearing a musket in his hand. He puts a lighted candle at the end of the barrel and waits until Harlequin has finished dancing. After he has shot him dead he retreats into the " wings," but Harlequin gets up and runs off to the opposite side. Now Scaramouch enters carrying a lantern to look at the dead body but, unable to find it, he turns away again. Harlequin quickly lies down midway across the stage. Scaramouch returns again without a lantern and falls headlong over Harlequin. He rises, takes hold of him, stands him stiffly on his feet and turns his head to and fro, sometimes forwards, sometimes backwards. Then he throws him over his leg and again stands him on his feet, picks him up on his back and carries him off ; and with this the air comes to an end. It should be observed that as soon as Harlequin is dead the Scaramouch air No. 26 is to be played.

31. Harlequin and his wife step forward as shown above. Now he runs round her with his usual movements and then she round him. Afterwards Harlequin goes to the extreme back of the stage and the woman to the extreme front, where she dances alone facing the audience with her back to the man. Then Harlequin beckons to the woman as if intimating they should go off, but she turns round and shows that she has no intention of doing so. Harlequin runs towards his wife and she to where he formerly stood. Afterwards Harlequin dances alone as

she did, and now she beckons to him in the same manner. Finally they approach each other, hold each other's left hand, draw their swords or bats, strike each other on the shoulder and exit.

32. Here is seen a blind man who, hearing the sound of music, sets his staff firmly on the ground and jerks his shoulders to and fro as if about to dance. But Harlequin enteres and crawling between his two feet throws his hat into his face. Then the blind man gropes about and strikes the air with his staff.

33. Harlequin creeps from under the blind man and, putting his hat on his bat, holds it in front of the face of the blind man, who, feeling himself touched, lashes out bravely with his staff. Thereupon Harlequin begins to laugh loudly and when he has performed divers strange *pas* from one side to the other they exit together.

34. Scapino dances alone executing, among other *pas*, his *ballonnés, chassés, contretemps* and *pas de rigaudon*, with his arms twisted from side to side. The air is played at will.

35. Enter Scapino and his wife, each going towards the other. They perform the *pas* noted in the previous dance. Then, back to back, they push each other several times as shown above and afterwards they walk off.

36. When the curtain rises there is seen this person, who performs certain *contretemps* with a drawing-up of the knees and feet. The rest of the necessary *pas* will be found in No. 34.

37. When Mezzetino and his wife have danced in the manner previously described, and used half their air, they perform the movement shown above, to the left and to the right. Then they run about several times with joined hands, and finally exit.

38. This buffoon does various foolish but curious *pas*, with distorted but comic jumps, which he varies as much as possible and endeavours to make still more humorous, until the air has been played three times.

39. The same buffoon performs the previous dance with

his wife, using the same *pas* as shown above ; and when they have performed it alternately, it is followed by other, different comical variations.

40. This person enters as shown above and dances in a circle after his own manner, and when, to the delight of the audience, he has performed strange, crooked and limping *pas*, the dance comes to an end.

41. In this dance the *pas* should be done as shown above, with varied turning movements. It should be observed that it is no different from the jumping about of the Marzochette in Purricinella's play, except that the dance must be executed in a beautiful manner.

42. Here Pantalone and his Pandora are at the ball. But since he is old she refuses to dance with him. Finally she grips his beard, turns him round in a circle, and, having done this several times, drags him off by his beard. The air is played twice.

43. This plate represents the Bolognese Doctor. He gravely dances peasant steps, but in a beautiful manner as if he were an old man. The air is played three times.

44. Both the Doctor and his wife take part in this scene and enter from opposite sides. She beckons to the Doctor who does not want to come and puts his hat on. Then he dances with her using informal, but unusual, peasant *pas* until the air has been played three times.

45. This approaching figure of Narcisino of Malembergo[1] has a straw hat on his head. His eyes are fashioned of fresh orange peel and his nose is made very comical by the addition of a piece of pumpkin. He dances *contretemps* and *ranzegnati ;*[2] that is, with drawn up knee and raised foot. Then he stands on one foot and now and again strikes the other foot against

---

[1] Malalbergo, a small town between Bologna and Ferrara.

[2] This word is probably derived from the Italian *rana*, meaning frog ; and is a frog-like movement. The direction " with drawn up knee and raised foot " suggests this.

the knee. Finally, he performs the *pas de rigaudon*, with wonderful contortions, and continues all manner of droll movements until the air comes to an end.

46. These two persons both run in and the man wants to kiss the woman, who turns away. As he becomes insistent she hits him with her hand, and then they dance quite merrily in the manner described.

47. At the beginning this person[1] stands on one foot, and after he has sufficiently retained the position, he dances from one side to the other and jumps about until the dance comes to an end. It can be repeated at pleasure.

48. Two persons dance the same air, each on opposite sides of the stage. As the woman turns her back, the man hits her lightly on the shoulder in a friendly way, and afterwards they continue with other *pas* of their own invention, according to the rules of the art.

49. Two buffoons fight with their feet, kicking forwards and backwards until the air has been played twice. And when it ends again they take off their hats and hit each other with them, twice in front and twice on the back, which brings the dance to an end.

50. These four persons enter with *cabrioles, pas de bourrée* and *contretemps* and then take the position shown. As the letters V.M.G.L., written on white cardboard, have been stitched on the crowns of their black hats, they hold them facing the audience until the sign " a " in the air is reached. Then they separate, using the previous *pas*, and repeat the same pose in a different manner, retaining it until the sign " b " is reached. This continues until the air has been played twice or three times. It should be noted that the bars " a " and " b " should be repeated each time they are encountered."[2]

---

[1] Fenocchio.

[2] The purpose of the letters c to h, also written above the air, is not explained.

Dieses ist die erste Positur, oder der Ansatz zu einer lincken Seit=Capriole, nach welcher eine andere, auf die rechte Seiten, folgen mus, die übrige Pas, als Pirole Rigaudon, Coupe ꝛc. sind aus der Vorrede herzuholen, worauf ein Jeder leicht, diesen Tantz völlig zu Componiren wissen wird.

Sarabande

Dieſer Tantz fänget ſich mit
einer Coupe an, worauf die pas Tombès
Siſon & Boure; folgen, das übrige von dieſer Sarabande, mag ein jeder
nach ſeinen belieben
machen

3

Payſane.

Dieſe Figur ſtellet den erſten Bauern Pas vor, auf welchen ein gleicher, jedoch mit den andern fuß verkehrter pas folget, wie die Figur zeiget, darauf ſeynd Pas di Contra-temps, u:rigaudon mit hin und wieder:Ziehung der Armen. Knie und beinen zu machen jedoch alles mit veränder, unge auf Bauern Arth.

Nach dem dieses vorstellende baar den halben tantz ge
macht, so schleicht die frau gemach hinweg, und da der
Mann sie nicht mehr siehet, fängt Er an zu weinen.
die Frau aber kömt unvermerckt wieder hinter ihm
her, fäßet Ihm bey den Schuldtern an, und drehet ihm
etlich mal herum, und weil Sie den Mann weinen siehet,
fangen sie aufs neu an zu tantzen.

Riguadon

Diesen Tantz fängt der Bauer allein an, u: zu Ende der
arin. Komt die frau mit einen besen herauß schläget u:
Jagt den Mann hinweg, dieser aber kehrt wieder zuruck,
u: wiedersetzt sich der frauen, da sie imer auf ihm loßge=
het u: vollbringen also gantz uneinig den tantz mit
unterschiedlichen Schlägen, u: lauffen beede davon

La disamecitia.

Hier komen Man und frau aufs Theatrum, u. trohen einander mit höltzernen Tellern, und da sie nach den
musical tact sich stets herumb drehen, schlagen sie die
Teller aneinander, und sobald sie sich hernachumbar-
met, u. die Teller weg geworfen, so hat der Tantz ein Ende.

Contadineta.

Dieser Tantz stelt ein verliebtes bauern Paar vor, welche beym
Anfang im Tantzen mit den Ellenbogen, und ferßen zusamen
stoßen, und hernach den tantz mit andern verschiedenen ac
tionen biß zu Ende der aria vollbringen als welche nach je,
des wohl gefallen 2 a. 3 mahl wiederhollet.

Paesant.

Hier werden 2 perfonen vorgeftellt, welche ei
nen freundfchaffts-tantz formiren, u: einander
nach deme fie fich mit ihren Hütten erfrifchet,
im Kopf kratzen, worbey fie die Schultern und
Beine, Wechfel-weiß gegen fich ziehen, und nach
allerhand Tact-mäßig gemachten lächerliche Po,
ßen, den tantz vollenden.

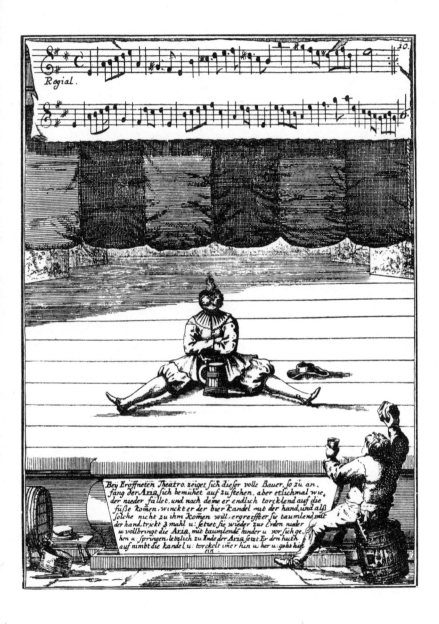

Ein voller bauer komt mit der Kandel torcklend herauß u:
nach dem die Aria einmahl zu End, nahet sich seine frau zu ihm
u: da Sie ihn also voll siehet, klopffet sie auß verwunderung
auf ihr Knie, der Mann aber reichet ihr zu trincken,
und nach dem Sie getruncken, Tantzen sie betruncken herumb, doch stellet sich die frau, alß ob sie noch nicht genug hät
te u tantzen also zusamen, biß sie sich endlich verliehren.

12

Zwey Bauer=Jungen fangen an zutantzen,
und wann die Aria zu Ende, komen Zwey Bauern und lachen jene im Nasen schneutzen aus,
u: daße kleinen ein gleiches gegen selbige gethan, schlagen die große mit den Ellenbogen u:
kniß die kleinen, dergleichen thun auch diese wechsel-
weiß denen großen, u: wollen also die größern, die Kleine-
re im tantz hintern, nach deme sie aber sich mit
einander verglichen, formiren sie alle vier den
tantz zusamen, und lauffen entlich mit frölichen ge-
behrden in die Bühne hinein.

Romagniola

Ein Romanischer Schiffer macht gewiſſe pas
Ballones, hinter ſich, und andere pas Boures vor ſich, und miſchet darunter mit verdrehung und Schwingung der Arme, einige
pas di Rigaudon, und Calles, nach
einmahlig getantzter Aria, begeben ſie
ſich wieder hinein.

Romagniola

Der vorige Schiffer tantzt mit seinem Weib auß der Scena her
aus und nach dem Er sie etlichmaln fangend, durch seine arme
passiren laßen wie die Figur außweiset, tantzen sie hernach
N° 13 gemelte Aria, und zwar eins gegen das andere, zu Ende der
Aria, umbarmen sie sich, und tantzen wieder hinein.

Hier komen zwey alte Weiber herauß, und tanzen halb gehend, halb zitterend aus euserste des Theatri, wan sie gantz vornen sind kratzen sie sich an Bauch und hintern, und Drehen sich herumb, dann kehren sie sich ruckwarts biß zum Anfang des Theatri, und machen eben diese gestus, wenn sie dort angekomen, Dieses hinter und vor sich gehen, Dauret biß zu Ende der Ersten Aria. währender dieser Zeit komt ein Jüngling aus der Scena, und da er dise alte Weiber siehet, lachet Er sie aus, und wan die Aria der Weiber ein Ende hat, nimbt er eine nach der andern bey der hand, und zerret sie beyden armen biß seine des Jünglings Aria, 2 oder 3 mahl getantzt worden Es ist aber zu mercken daß dieser Tantz in 2 Arien bestehet deren die Erste langsam andere aber lustig oder geschwind gehet.

N'oudle Fantastiche

Diese zwey Mascheren, presentiren 4 Persohné
so gravitétisoh, und gleichsam mit Mühe, von einer
zur andern Seiten, bald vor, bald hintersioh, bald in die
runde tantzen, der gestalt daß es scheint als ob jeder
noch einen andern Menschen auf den rucken triege, und
dieses währet so lang, als es dem Tantzer gefällig

17

Satyro

Ein Satyrus macht pas Ballones, so lang biß die violin in
der Aria zum Zeichen △ komt, als den so blaset der Satyr
seine Orgel u. accompagniret die violin zugleich, u.
die Frau spielet mit gleichen Accord auf der Cimbano
wan nun obiges Zeichen verbey, so fanget Er wieder
anzutantzen, wen aber das Zeiche □ komt
fangen sie auch wieder mit der Orgel und
Cimbano unter streichender Violin an zu
blaßen u: zu spielen, u: zwar so offt sie zu
denen Zeichen komen, die Aria kan
nach belieben gemacht werde, so lang man
will

E

Dieser masquirte Bauer, stehet in einem korb ohne boden
und machet die pas riguadon, mit starcken fuß stampfen
auf die Erde, hernach machet Er obengezeigte Figur mit
pas ballones et contretemps auf bäurerische aber kunst
mäßige art, und wird darbej die Aria 4 mahl abgespielt

Hier præsentirt sich ein Mann mit 2. Gesichtern. Erstlich vorwerts stäts
gen Himmel schauend, und fängt an mit Capriolen Piroleten, und andere Spanischen pas zutantzen hernach stelt er sich hinterwerts dar
und weist sein anders Gesicht, benebst dass er in solcher Kleidung
wie vorwerts erscheinet, und macht ebenfalls dergleichen
verschiedene Caprioln, und gehet zu Ende
der 5 mahl gespielten
Aria hinein.

20

Eben dieselbe Figur, kommt mit samt der Frau, eines auf dieser,
daß ander auf der andern seite herauß, und tantzen alsobald
mit zusamen geschlossenen händen und drehen die köpff imer
hin ü: her, dañ sie geschwind wieder auß einander lauffen, daß
machen sie wechsel weiß, bald geschlossen, bald jedes gantz allei,
die Aria wird treÿ mahl gespielt.

Ein Romaner macht eine Capriola vor sich,
und flugs eine hinter sich, wie auch von Einer Seiten zur andern, Im übrgen wird ein jeder selbst einige schöne Inventionen mit frantzöischen pas
formiren, die Aria wird 3 mahl
gespielt.

Corente

Hier werden in Romanischen habit,
die pas Corrente, Bouré und Ciacone
mit hüpscher bewegung der Arme, deß
Haubts und des Leibs gedantzt und die
Aria 2 mahl gespielt.

Scaramuzza

forte   piano   forte

Bej Öffnung des Theatri, præsentirt sich diese lächerliche Figur, zu hinderst der Schaubühne, und kommet alsdan gantz gemach hervor und machet mit Erhöh: u: verlängerung seiner, eine natürliche gestalt und wirfft hierauff den Mantel hinter sich springt mit geraden füßen etwas in die höhe, und spreist folgends die füße auß einander so weit als im mer möglich, u: kömet stracks wieder mit graden füßen zu stehen. Nach diesen allen macht Er gantz gemach lange Scaramutza Schritt, mit cappri olen, auf unterschiedliche Manier, biß zu End der Ariæ.

24

Lours.

Bey eröffneten Theatro præsentirt sich diese
schöne unbewegliche Statua, biß der erste Theil der
Aria gespielt, bey wiederholung derselben, springt
der Scaramuza vom fuß Gestell, und machet seine
schöne Scaramuza pas. mit Capriolē u. Piroleten
nach 5. mahl gespielter Aria hat der tantz ein
ende

Gran Alesandro.

Wie diese Figur vorstelt, so kombt der Scara=
mutza herauß, und macht große Schritt mit
Capriolen u: Piroleten vermischt, und tantzt
solcher gestalt, wie zum öftern schon der Unter=
richt hirvon gegeben worden

26

Scaramuza.

forte   piano   forte

Der Scaramutza kombt mit zweyen körben herauß. worinnen zwey
kleine Scaramutzen seyn. ü. setzet solche auf die Erden. ü. nachdeme
Er eine gantze Aria außgetantzt. eröfnet die kleinen Scaramutzen
die korb. da er nun selbige siehet. erstaunet er darüber. diese aber springe
auß den korben ü. geben Scaramutza eins mit den fuße vor den hintern. ü. werffen Ihm zu boden. dan tantzen die kleinen Scaramutzē
die gantze Aria allein. hernach nimbt der wieder aufgestandene Scaramutz
za. eine nach der andern. ü. jagt sie wieder in die korb hinein. und hierbey
Endigt sich die helffte der Aria. bey der andern helffte nimbt Er die
korb ü. geht mit langen Schritten hinein

27

Scaramuzza e Donna

Diese zwey Perſohnen ſpringẽ wann der erſte Theil
der Aria zu Ende, aus der Scena heraus, und ſo
beÿ Anfang des andern Theils wieder zuruck ſtel-
len nachfolgende artige Figur vor.

Von dieser Figur siehet man nichts anders, alß den Huth und Fuß, und wann die **Aria** 3. od. 4. mahl gespilt ändern sie die Figur, und nehmen wieder die erste Stellung an mit unterschiedlichen Caprioln, alsdan verlaßen sie den Schauplatz.

Chicona.

Arlequin, komt wie dieße ſchöne Figur zeiget herauß, und fanget
Schritt vor Schritt an, auf ſeine Manier zu tantzen, dan naket ſich
der Scaramutza mit einer Latern zu ihm, tantzt und äffet den
Arlequin, reſolvirt ſich aber endlich hinweg zugehen.

Chicona

Scaramutzo kombt, mit einer flinde in der hand, ü: zwar mit seinen Mantel gantz be
deckt heraus, ü: setzt auf die Spitze des rohrs ein brenend licht, wartet biß Arlequin ausgedantzt,
nach deme er ihn tod geschossen, rederirt er sich in die Scena, Arlequin aber stehet wieder
auf, ü: laufst auf der andern seide auch hinein, indeß kombt Scaramutza, mit der in handen
habendē Laterne herauß, umb den todten zu sehen, allein da er ihn nicht findet, kehrt er
wieder hinweg, Arlequin aber legt sich geschwind vor die Scena im weg, alß nun Scara=
mutza ohne Latern aufs Neue wieder kombt, fallt Er Sturtzbaumēnt über Arlequin, steh,
et wieder auf, nimbt denselben hernach ü: stelt Ihm gantz steiff auf die süß, wendet Ihm
den kopff hin ü: wieder, bald vor= bald hintersich, hernach wirfft Er Ihm über seinē fuß,
und stellt ihm nochmahls auf die füße, faßt als den solchen auf seinen rücken, tragt Ihn
hinweg, und hiemit Endigt sich die Aria ;
Es ist aber zu mercken, daß so bald der Arlequin tod ist, so spielt
man di Aria deß Scaramutza.
Nº 76.

Chicoha

Arlequin ü. sein weib stellen obige figur schritt
var schritt vor, hernach laufft der Arlequin mit seinen
gewohnlichē bewegungen um daß weib herumb, ü. die frau u. den
man. dan begiebt sich Arlequin in daß hinderste ü. die frau auf
daß vorderste des Theatri ü. tantzt gantz allein mit dē gesicht gegē
die zuschauer. ü. den rucken gegen den man wendend, alß da winck
et Arlequin der fraue. eben alß wen sie beyde hinein gehē wolten.
allein sie wendet sich um. ü. bezeuget daß sie keine lust hierzu ha
be, da laufft der Arlequin gegen daß weib, und die an daß ort
wo Arlequin geßtanden. dan tantzet Arlequin wie vorher daß
weib allein, welche ihm gleichfals wie er gethan wincket:
endlich nahen sie sich zusamen, ü. faßen einander bey
der lincken hand. ziehen ihre Batalch oder Hotzē
herauß ü. schlagen einander auf die schulter und
gehen hinein.

Hier stelt man einen Blinden vor, der als Er Musi-
ciren hort, seinen Stock fest auf die Erden Pflantzt,
ū: die achsel hin ū: her zuckt gleich ob er anfangen wolt
zu tantzen, Arlequin aber kombt herauß, und kreucht
den blinden zwischen die füße, ū: schmeist ihm mit den
hut ins gesicht, der blinde aber tappet hierauff umb sich,
und schlägt mit seinen Stock in
die lufft

33

Arlequin kräugt unter den blinden hervor, setzt
seinen hut auf die britsche ü: hält solchen den blinden
vors gesicht, dieser so bald er sich berührt vermerck
et, schlägt mit seinen stock wacker umb sich herum,
worüber der *Arlequin* laut anfängt zu lachen, ü: nach
dem Er unterschiedliche *Curseule* pas, von einer
seiten zur andern gemacht, gehen sie beede miteinander hine in.

G

Scapin tantzt allein u̇. macht unter andern ſeine pas ballonés
Schafes-contretemps, u̇. rigaudon mit hin und wieder gedreheten
armen, und wird die Arie nach belieben geſpielt.

Scapin und sein Weib, kommen und zwar eins gegen den
andern heraus, und machen die bey vorhergehenden Tantz
alschon angezeigte pas. Endlich stoßen sie, wie obige Figur
vorstellt, unterschiedliche mahl mit den rücken aneinander, und marchiren soden
hinweg

Bey Eröffnung der Bühne Præsentiret sich diese Figur,
welche im herauß gehen gewiße Contretemps mit
ziehung der knie und füße macht, die übrige
nöthige pas aber sind N:̊ 34 zu finden.

Nach dem Mezzetin und sein weib, auf Erst=
besagte weiße getantzt ü: die halbe Aria zu Ende
gebracht mache sie wechsel weiße die oben vorgestellte
Figur, lincks ü: rechts, ü: lauffen hernach mit geschlossenen
händen, etliche mahl herumb, ü: folgends gar hinweg.

Dieß Narren-Figur macht unterschiedliche närrische
doch Curieuse pas. mit unform aber lächerliche springen
ü: verändert solche, aufs possierlichste so viel imer
möglich, biß die Arie 3 mahl gespielt worden.

Mato.

Vorbeschrie-
ner Narr. macht mit
seinen weib den vorigen
Tantz. u: zwar mit selbigen
pas, wie obige Figur zeiget,
ü: wan sie es wechsel weiß
vollbracht, so volgen hernach
unteschiedliche andere
lächerliche ver-
änderungen.

Gobba e Stropio.

Dieße Figur kombt wie hier oben zusehē heraus,
ū: nach deme sie auf ihre Manier in einen kreiß
herumb getantzt, ū: nach sonderēr krummer und
unekender pas gemacht, endigt sich zu aller zu
schauer vergnügen der Tantz.

Bei diesen Tantz soll man, wie obige Figur
weist, diejenige Pas mit unterschiedlichen wendungen gegen
einander Observiret, gestalten er nicht anderst, den wie die
Scaramouchetten im Pulcinellæ Spiel, herum springen
gemacht wird, jedoch, so damit der Tantz auf eine schöne
Manier, möge vorgestellt werden.

Meo ho Barba Nicolo.

Hier findet sich Pantalon mit seiner Pandora beym Tantz
ein, weiln er aber alt, so weigert sie sich etlichmahl mit Ihm zu
tantzē, endlich ergreifft sie seinen barth ū: drehet Ihm ver=
schiedene mahl im Creiß herumb, ū: nach sothanen offtern
herumb drehen, wann die Aria 2 mal gespielt,
so schleppet sie selben beym barth hinein

Bolognesa

Beÿ dieser vorstellung komt der Doctor mit seiner
Frauen, u: zwar eins gegé dem andern heraust, u:
winckt die Frau den Doctor, allei er will nicht ko̅
men, sonder setzt seinen hut auf u: tantzt mit der
Frauē unförmliche aber Curiese bäurische pas
biß die Aria 3 mahl gespiehlt worden.

Narcisin

Diese komen alle beÿde lauffent herauß, ü: will der mann
daß weib küßen, allein sie drehet sich mit verkehrtē leib
von Jhm hinweg, und in deme er sich zu vergnügen be-
müht schlägt Jhm daß weib mit der hand, und vollführ-
en hernach gantz lustig auf vorbesagte weiße ihr-
en Tantz.

Diese Figur stehet anfänglich nur auf einen fuß und wan sie sich in eine gute positur gestellet, tantzet sie hernach von einer seite zur andern und springt herumb, biß die Aria zu Ende, Man kan sie nach Jedes belieben ver= doppeln.

48

Zwey Persohnen
tantzē außerhalb dem *Theatro,* dieselbe *Aria* eine
auf dieser die andre auf der ander seite, u: in dē daß
weib den ruckē wendet, schlägt sie der mañ gantz freundlich
auf die achsel. u: tantzē hernach solcher gestallt wie ein jeder nach
seine wohlgefallē selbst erfinden kan, oder etwaß kunst
mäßiges vor zu   stellen weiß.

Riguadon

Zweÿ Schalcks narrn-Aff.
ron tiern einander, mit fuſſe
vor den hinder ſtoſſende, wähend da die Aria
zweÿ mal geſpiehlt wird, u: wañ ſie zum
andeᷓ mal zu Ende, nimt bald dieſer bald
jener dē huth, u: ſchlagē einander zweÿ
mal vor, u: zweÿ mal hinter ſich, u:
hiemit Endet ſich der Tantz

I

PART TWO

Sig. Greg: Lambranzi
Maestro di Balli.

NEUE und CURIEUSE
THEATRIALISCHE
TANTZ-SCHUL
Zweyter theil,
Nürnberg, verlegt von
Joh. Jacob Wolrab.

Part Two

A Description of the Plates

1. This plate explains the manner of performing a *cabriole* upwards. Then follow *pas graves*, *pas de bourrée*, *pas tombés*, *pas de sissonne*, *balancés*, *pas de rigaudon* and *pas de chaconne* until the air has been played twice.

2. This dance begins with *coupés*, *piroles* [*pirouettes*?] and *pas graves*. The continuation can be arranged by the dancers themselves who, by means of curious variations, can devise beautiful figures. The air is played twice.

3. A Venetian merchant performs the previously mentioned dance according to the gondolier plate No. 5. And when the air has been played twice the dance ends.

4. The same merchant dances with his wife the measure No. 5. It concludes when the air has been played twice.

5. Enter a Venetian boatman or gondolier who dances a *Furlana* in the Venetian manner, which contains a particular version of the usual *pas*, and continues until the air has been played two or three times.

6. Here the gondolier and his wife perform the previous Venetian dance. But they alter the figures and *pas* so that they alternately execute the *chassés* in a circle. When the air has been played twice they are lost to view.

7. This Switzer performs the whole of the pike exercise and dances after the manner of his country. But one must be

well versed in the use of the pike. The air can be repeated as often as required.

8. This Switzer dances in the manner already described and at the same time waves the standard and does all the motions. The air is played ten, eleven, or more times when the performer is able to perform these momevents.

9. This dance is performed by six people dressed as statues. At the beginning they make a wide covered archway, through which the gardener dances forwards. Afterwards they change the arches into characteristic figures and finally form a circle, and when the gardener stands in the middle of it the curtain is lowered.

10. A Dutch sailor enters sadly, with his hands held under his arms as if he were freezing. He bows twice and then begins to dance quite unusual *pas* until the air has been played twice.

11. The sailor dances with his wife and they alternately strike their hands together, one into the other's, and perform a similar movement with their feet. Afterwards they dance in their own manner and exit when the air has been played twice.

12. These three persons remain motionless until the air has been played once. When it is repeated and the sign " A " is reached, those at each side jump to the ground and assume another pose as shown in the next plate.

13. When the sign " B " is reached they turn apart and take the position shown in the next plate.

14. Thus they stand, rigid, only slightly changing their position at each musical beat or bar. But as soon as the sign " C " is reached they jump apart again.

15. This is the third pose. And when the violin comes to the sign " D " they assume this pose.

16. And when the sign " E " is reached they take this position.

17. And thus they remain, rigid, until the sign " F " is reached, when the dance comes to an end.

N.B.—This is but one dance with the changes described.

The centre statue remains motionless until the dance comes to an end.

18. Two persons enter from one side and two from the other. Each holds a spit in his hands. Clever inventions will make this dance attractive.

19. Here is the second part of the dance. The air is played twice.

20. In the above plate two persons carry in Bacchus and hold him up until the air ends. Then they set him down and dance the following beautiful dance.

21. Here two persons beat their staves together at top and bottom, as well as behind. They continue this several times in different ways and then carry off Bacchus.

22. A dancer, dressed as an English sailor and hung with wooden spoons, jumps in with a big *cabriole*, and continues to dance to and fro with curious but correct *cabrioles*, until the air has been played twice.

23. These two persons enter from the " wings " with *ballonnés*. The man kisses his two fingers, places the kisses on the palm of his other hand and blows them into the woman's apron ; she tries to catch them in it. The dance is performed with *ballonnés* and the air is played six times.

24. Here is a wooden statue which has been covered with pieces of stone, made to adhere by means of plaster, so that it appears shapeless. It is set upon the stage. Then enter two sculptors who chisel the statue as they dance, so that the pieces of stone fall off and the mass is transformed into a statue. The *pas* can be arranged at pleasure. The air is played twice.

25. Two blacksmiths forge a nail in time with the music until the air has been played once. Then one lays down his hammer and dances *chassés*, *ballonnés*, *pirouettes*[1] and *pas de rigaudon* until the air has been repeated ; meanwhile the other one forges. Finally they both dance together and exit.

[1] The German is *Birollets*, the B would appear to be a mistake for P.

26. Two coopers are seen who drive hoops on a barrel in time with the music. Each time a hoop is driven on, they dance round the barrel. When it is completed they roll it off. The dance can be arranged at pleasure.

27. When the curtain is raised a tailor is seen, sitting at work on a bench. When the air has been played once, he puts his work away and dances in the Venetian manner for as long as he pleases.

28. The same tailor, while dancing, measures a young woman for a dress. When this is done they both dance together in the Venetian manner as in No. 4 [No. 5 ?].

29. A cobbler is seen with the tools of his trade, the use of which he expresses in mime. He prepares the thread by hanging it on the wall and rubbing it with cobbler's wax, in time with the music.

The dancer who can successfully imitate these actions is to be commended.

30. Here stands the cobbler preparing his thread for use. Meanwhile his wife enters and they dance together with familiar *pas*.

31. Enter a sportsman with his musket. He loads his weapon, shoots a bird and plucks it. Then he cuts a stake on which he threads the bird and makes a fire over which he roasts it. Afterwards he eats the bird. The air is continued until all this has been mimed.

32. Two tennis players enter from opposite sides. As they dance they hit the ball with their rackets, in the usual manner of the game. The air is played three or four times.

33. This is the first posture taken by four grenadiers, who immediately go through the whole of their drill while they dance. They shoulder arms and turn half-left, half-right and so on.

34. In this second plate they present arms and so continue until the exercise is ended.

35. This plate represents a person who enters and jumps

4

against the wall, and in turning assumes the position shown in the next plate. Afterwards he performs *cabrioles* to right and left, backwards and forwards, also while turning, so that the dance really consists of nothing but masterly jumps.

36. This shows the jump after the turn, which must be done very quickly. The air is played three times.

37. The dancer, as shown in the plate, continually performs *pas piroles* [?] and jumps quickly upwards, and then executes more *pas piroles*.

38. Four Turks enter, one after the other, and dance with joined hands as shown; backwards, forwards, and to right and left, with *ballonnés* and other suitable *pas*. The air is played three times.

39. Enter two negroes, accompanied by a Turkish dwarf who beats a drum in time with the music. Then the negroes take each other's sash and wind it round themselves. And after clapping their hands together they turn round with *pas pirole*[1] [*pirouettes*?] and *ballonnés*, always keeping in profile as shown, until, after various *contretemps*, the air has been played three times.

40. Enter two galley slaves, chained together, who perform *pas* appropriate to the dance. But the hands must be kept clasped to avoid falling to the ground.

41. This person does a great many different contortions, with furious and quick jumps, until the air has been played twice.

42. Enter two persons carrying ladders on their shoulders; one from the right, one from the left side. They place the ladders together as shown above, and when one has climbed up and tumbled through the rungs, head downwards to the ground, the first performance is at an end.

43. Then this pose is taken and the same tumbles and jumps are done.

[1] The German word is *pas Birolle*.

44. Afterwards the dance continues in this manner, as long as required, then changes to the pose shown in the next plate.

45. A somersault from back to front.

46. Afterwards the above movement is done, which represents the trundling of a wheel-barrow, then follows :—

47. This pose, in which two persons have joined the previous couple. They change as follows :—

48. They jump apart and three of them raise the fourth in the air, by his hands and feet, and carry him off. Therefore the dance is ended.

49. A gypsy, playing castanets, dances a solo *Chaconne*, with *ballonnés* and *pas de bourrée*, combined with *contretemps*, *balancés* and *pirouettes*,[1] until the air is concluded. Enter a necromancer who touches her with his wand ; she becomes rigid. Afterwards he dances alone and finally they both dance together to the end.

50. Two persons, wearing witch masks, dance with crouched bodies. Now comes a person, wearing a ghost mask, whom they fling over their arms. Then they perform droll jumps to right and left, and exit.

51. This represents the first lesson. The dancing-master should demonstrate the first *pas*, taking the right foot then the left, the knees being kept straight, then bent and again straightened.

---

[1] The German word is *Pirolleten*.

Vidali.

Diese Figur zeiget hauptsächlich an, wie man
eine Capriol gerade in die höhe machen soll
darauf folgen pas = graues, boures, tumbes
Sissoni, Ballancemens, Rigaudons, und pas
di Chacona, so lang, bis die Aria 2. mahl
abgespielt worden.

L

Dimo de sü

Ein Venedischer Kaufman stelt eben
vorberührten Tantz wie beym Gonde-
heur N. angemercket vor, und
hat, wann die Aria zweymahl
gespielt, der Tantz ein
Ende

Suzzero

Dieser Schweitzer macht alle Exerci-
tia mit der Pique und tantzt nach seiner Landes art, es muß sich aber
einer zu vor mit der Pique wohl
exerciren, die Aria kan man spielen
so offt man will

Gärtiniera

Dieser Tantz wird von 6. als Statuen gekleidete Personen formirt, machen in anfang einen weiten bedeckten
gang, dann komt unter disen der Gärtner tantzend hervor, hernach verändern sie die bögen in unterschidliche Fi-
guren, und letzlich machen einen runden bogen, und
wann der Gärtner miten darinn still: stehet, wird
der Vorhang herunter gelaßen.

M

Genio

Gemelter Schiffer tanzt mit seiner Frauen und Schlagen wechselsweiß die Hände in einander Ein solches
verrichten sie auch mit den Fussen, und
Danzten hernach ihrer Manier, wan die Aria
2. mahl gespielt, gehen sie ab.

Statue

Diese 3 Figurn, bleiben immer unbeweglich stehen,
biß die Aria zu Ende, und wann solche zum an-
dernmahl an gefangen, und zum Zeichen A. kombt
springen die beider — seits stehende zur Erden, und machen die — folgende Figur

detto.

und wann der Tantz beym Zeichen E. ist, zei, get sich denn folgende Figur.

Galiardo.

Einem Englischen Schiffers Habit mit
Holtzernen Löffeln behangen, Springet mit einer
Grossen Capriolen herauß u: Continuirt der
Gesang mit Curieusen regelmässigen Capriolen
biß zu Endt, biß die Aria 3 mahl gespielet
worden.

24

Archi teto

Hier wird eine Hölzerne Statua, durch hülffe
deß Kalchs angeklebten Stuckg: Steinen überzo,
gen, und auff Theatro gestelt damit sie unförmlich
aussieht, dan komen 2 Bildhauer herauß
Schlagen tantzend an die Statue, so fällen die
Steine herauß, da dan die Figur, so eine Statua
erkand wird, die pas kan jedes nach beliebet
machen, u. wird die Aria 2 mahl gespielt.

Zwey Schmiede schmieden einen
Nagel nach dem Mufiialischen Tact, biß die
Aria einm: zu ende, dan legt der Eine den Hamer nie-
der, u: tanst die pas Cafse, Ballones, Birolleti und
rigaudon, biß die aria zum andern mahl zu ende,
danzt der andere, und der Erste Schmidet, entlich tanzen fie beijde miteinander und gehen
alsdan hinein.

26

Zwey Bütner Präsentiren sich und
legen nach dem Musicalischen Tact, reif=
fen ein Vas, und tantzen so offt, ein reiff
angetrieben wird. Wie selbiges, wan das
Vas fertig drehen sie es hinein in
die Manier der pas kan jsie
nach besten lieben Comooo
ren

Salorini

Eben dieser Schneider, nimt untern tanz,
einer Jungfer das Maaß zum kleid, wan
dieses geschehen, tanzen beÿde miteinan,,
der Venetianisch, wie bey Numro t.
zusehen.

Birgamasco

Ein Schuster Presentiret sich mit seinem Handwercks Marterialien, und stelt die verrichtung
des Handwercks in Figurn vor, Verfertigt
dem Schuhdrat, streicht ihm an Beÿwahr
mit dem pech, alles nach den Musicalischen
Tact; wer es accurat vorzustellen
weiß, der hat Lob davon.

30

Hier steht d' Schuster, richtet seinen
drat zum arbeiten zu recht
Indeme komt seine Frau, alsda
Dantzen die beÿde d' n Dantz
mit gewohnlichen pas.

rigadon

Es kombt ein Jäger mit seiner Büchsen heraus, und nach deme er sie geladen, schiesst er einen Vogel, rupffet ihn, Schniz et an einen Spieß, steckt dem Vogel dran, schlagt feuer, brät und isset solchen.
Aria wirt gespielt biß alles vorgestelt worden.

Zwey Rageten Spieler, komen dieß und jen
seits heraus schlagen, wehren den Tantz mit
der Racketen den Ball, nach arth wie es
im Spiel gebräuchlich, die aria wird
3. oder 4 mahl gespielt.

In der 2ten Figur, præsentiren sie
daß Gewöhr, u. wird so fort gefahren
bis zu end des Exercitii.

Saltz in Muro

Diese Figur repraesentirt eine Person, welche,
aus denen Scenen herauskomt, springt an d' Wandt,
und macht in der verdrehung volgede Figur, hernach
folgen Capriolen, rechts u: lincks, hinter und vorsich,
auch in die runde, das also der Ball mit lau-
ter Meistersprüngen gemacht wird.

dieses ist die vorige Figur und Stelt ein
Sprung in der verwendung vor, so aber
geschwind geschehen, die aria wird 3 mal
gespielt.

Als diese Figur zeigt, macht man alle,,
zeit, pas piroles, und springt geschwind
in die höhe und macht alsdan die pas piro,,
les nochmahl!

Animaria

Zwey mit Ketten geschlossene Sclaven kö=
men herauß, u. machen zu festen Tanth
durch die pas, es müssen aber die Hände
geschlossen bleiben, sonst fält man
zu Boden.

Desegnio Furia

Die hier vorgestelte Figur, machet sehr unterschiedliche verdrehungen, mit furiosen und geschwinden Sprüngen, so lang biß die Aria zwey-mahl gespielt.

Dann presentiret man diese figur und wer
den dabey eben die Sturtz-baum und
Spring gemacht

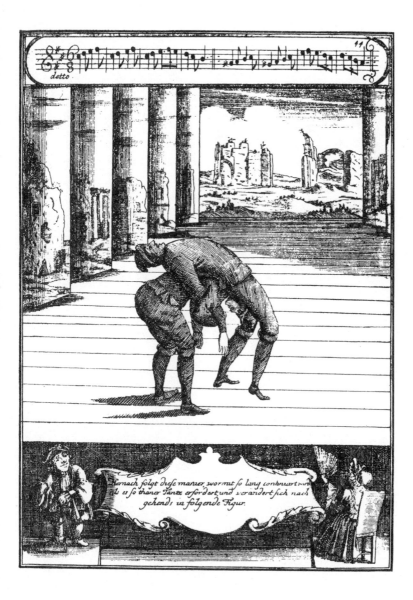

Ein Sturtzbaum von hinten vorwärts,
und wann die figur gemacht.

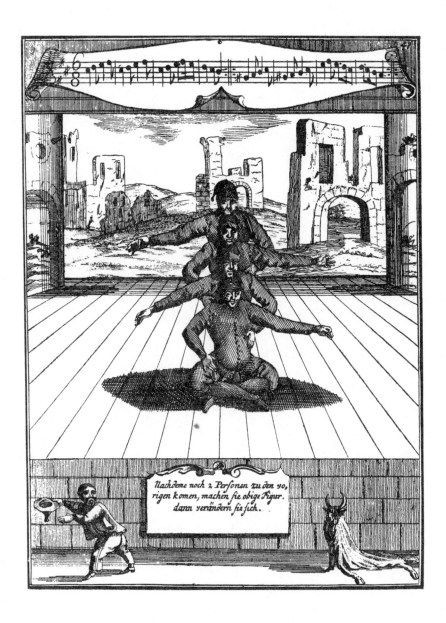

Nachdeme noch 2. Personen zu den vo,
rigen komen, machen sie obige Figur.
dann verändern sie sich.

Dann springen sie von einander, und ihrer drey heben den 4ten bey Händ und füssen in die Höhe, tragen ihm also hinein, hat also der ganze tantz ein Ende.

Cicona

eine Zigeunerin tantzt mit Castagnetten in der
Hand gantz allein eine Cicona mit pa Ballonè, Boures, u: vermengten Contratemps Ballancemengu: Pirro-
leten, biß die Aria einmahl zu end. Dann komt ein
Schwartzkünstler berühret sie mit dem Stock, da blebt sie stehen, alsden tantzt er allein, endlich tantzen beide mit einander biß   zu Endt.

R

Dieses ist die erste Lection, so ein Tantzmeister,
weiset, wie man mit dem rechten Fuß den ersten pas
gantz gerade gebogen und wieder aufgericht machen sol,
wie auch mit dem lincken, wie obige Figur außweist